Shady
The River Red Gum

Written and illustrated by

Angus Cameron

Published by Brolga Publishing Pty Ltd

ABN 46 063 962 443

PO Box 452

Torquay 3228 VIC

Australia

email: markzocchi@brolgapublishing.com.au

ISBN: 978-1-7640776-6-8

Printed in China
Cover design by Luke Harris, WorkingType Studio
Typeset by WorkingType Studio

To my children and grandchildren who teach me new things every day.

Shady the river red gum lives by a creek in the Australian bush. To find Shady you drive out of the city, along the highway, down a lane, across the paddock and to the creek.

Shady has a big trunk, long slender leaves, gumnuts, flowers and seeds. Shady has lots of friends! Let's meet them.

Kooka the kookaburra likes to sit in Shady's branches and laugh early in the morning and late in the evening. Kooka lives with his family. They blend into Shady's branches, so they are hard to see.

Can you make a sound like a kookaburra?

Who else will we find in Shady's branches?

Buzzy bees like to gather sweet nectar from Shady's flowers when the weather is warm. They make the nectar into the honey that you spread on your toast.

Can you make the sound of a buzzy bee?

Who else will we find in Shady's branches?

Maggie the magpie likes to sit in Shady's branches and sing songs. Maggie has a mate for life and together they build sturdy nests for their babies.

Can you sing like Maggie the magpie?

Who else will we find in Shady's branches?

Cocky the cockatoo makes a nest in Shady's hollow branches. Cockatoos have strong beaks to crack open nuts and seeds. They like to call loudly when they are flying around.

Can you screech like Cocky the cockatoo?

Who else will we find in Shady's branches?

Cory the corella likes to land in the very top branches and sleep there at night. Corellas like to gather in flocks and show off to each other. They love doing crazy tricks like hanging upside down before they go to sleep.

Can you flap your wings like Cory the corella?

Who else will we find in Shady's branches?

Spotty the pardalote is a tiny little bird with white spots. Spotty flits among Shady's branches eating insects from the leaves. This helps Shady stay healthy and strong. Spotty is hard to see but you can listen for his song.

What is your favourite birdsong?

Who else will we find in Shady's branches?

Willa the wallaby has dark brown fur and a white stripe on her face. She is a marsupial with a pouch for her baby. A baby wallaby is called a joey. Willa the wallaby likes to eat the grass around Shady at night. During the day she rests underneath Shady's branches.

Can you hop around like Willa the wallaby?

Who else will we find in Shady's branches?

Poppy the possum loves to eat Shady's leaves and flowers at night. Poppy can jump from branch to branch. She has soft fur and a lovely warm pouch for her babies to snuggle in.

Can you curl up and cuddle like Poppy the possum?

Who else will we find in Shady's branches?

Can you find Shady's friends?

Kooka the kookaburra

Buzzy bees

Maggie the magpie

Cocky the cockatoo

Cory the corella

Spotty the pardalote

Willa the wallaby

and

Poppy the possum?

Be Published

Publish through a successful publisher.

Brolga Publishing is represented through:

- National book trade distribution, including sales, marketing & distribution through Simon & Schuster.
- International book trade distribution to:
  - The United Kingdom
  - Sales representation in South East Asia
- Worldwide e-Book distribution

For details and enquiries, contact: